Read All About
FOOTBALL

by Colette Weil Parrinello

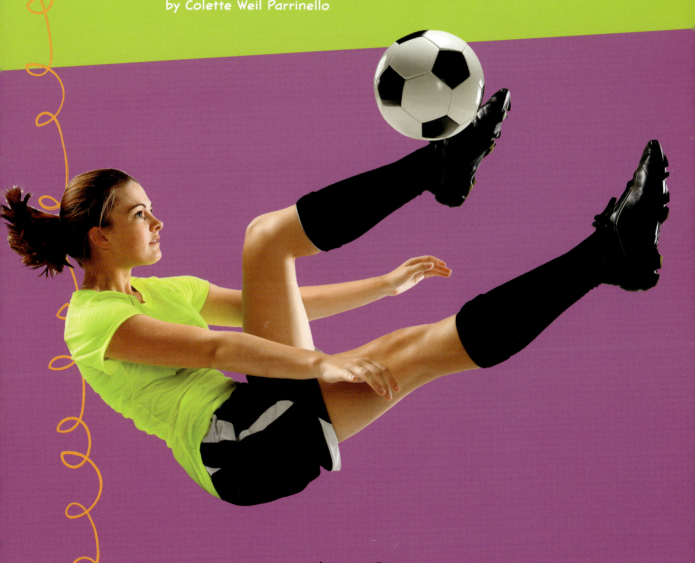

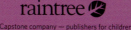

a Capstone company — publishers for children

Raintree is an imprint of Capstone Global Library Limited, a company incorporated in England and Wales having its registered office at 264 Banbury Road, Oxford, OX2 7DY – Registered company number: 6695582

www.raintree.co.uk
myorders@raintree.co.uk

Hardback edition © Capstone Global Library Limited 2024
Paperback edition © Capstone Global Library Limited 2025
The moral rights of the proprietor have been asserted.

All rights reserved. No part of this publication may be reproduced in any form or by any means (including photocopying or storing it in any medium by electronic means and whether or not transiently or incidentally to some other use of this publication) without the written permission of the copyright owner, except in accordance with the provisions of the Copyright, Designs and Patents Act 1988 or under the terms of a licence issued by the Copyright Licensing Agency, 5th Floor, Shackleton House, 4 Battle Bridge Lane, London SE1 2HX (www.cla.co.uk). Applications for the copyright owner's written permission should be addressed to the publisher.

Edited by Carrie Sheely
Designed by Bobbie Nuytten
Original illustrations © Capstone Global Library Limited 2024
Picture research by Donna Metcalf
Production by Tori Abraham
Originated by Capstone Global Library Ltd

978 1 3982 5130 4 (hardback)
978 1 3982 5131 1 (paperback)

British Library Cataloguing in Publication Data
A full catalogue record for this book is available from the British Library.

Acknowledgements
We would like to thank the following for permission to reproduce photographs: Alamy: Cal Sport Media, 27, FLHC 1111, 6, Frankie Angel, middle 30, REUTERS/MIKE BLAKE, bottom right 13, Xinhua, bottom right 19; Associated Press: AP Photo, bottom left 29, Martin Mejia, bottom left 15; Getty Images: ADRIAN DENNIS, 24, David Price, top left 22, Goddard_Photography, top right 23, Koichi Kamoshida, top right 30, RTimages, 14, Thomas Niedermueller, top right 25; Newscom: Top Photo Group, top right 5; Shutterstock: A.PAES, bottom right 21, Alizada Studios, top left 18, bottom right 18, Amy Myers, top right cover, Anatoliy Lukich, 26, Anton_Ivanov, bottom left 16, artnana, bottom right 5, BearFotos, bottom 22, Christian Bertrand, top right 9, middle right 17, Cosmin Iftode, top left 11, cristiano barni, top right 15, Fabrizio Andrea Bertani, 12, middle right 16, Gino Santa Maria, 1, middle 10, GIROMIN STUDIO, bottom left 11, Gorodenkoff, 8, Ground Picture, middle left 7, JoeSAPhotos, middle left 9, lazyllama, middle left 5, Lutsenko_Oleksandr, top right 29, Master1305, 20, Maxisport, bottom right 9, Mikolaj Barbanell, top right 19, mspoint, middle right 15, Natursports, middle right 11, Nirat.pix, bottom cover, Paolo Bona, top left 10, ricochet64, 28, Rose Carson, top right 17, Vasyl Shulga, middle right 13, top left 21, Ververidis Vasilis, bottom left 17, Vitalii Vitleo, top right 13, Yuri Turkov, bottom left 23; Wikimedia: The FA, top right 7

Every effort has been made to contact copyright holders of material reproduced in this book. Any omissions will be rectified in subsequent printings if notice is given to the publisher.

Printed and bound in India.

Contents

Chapter 1
History of football 4

Chapter 2
Playing on a pitch. 8

Chapter 3
Players and positions 12

Chapter 4
Teams 16

Chapter 5
Fans and stadiums 20

Chapter 6
Mascots and nicknames 24

Chapter 7
The World Cup 28

Glossary 31
Index 32
About the author 32

Words in **bold** are in the glossary.

Chapter 1

History of football

Football is one of the oldest sports. In ancient times, people played games that were like football. Today, football is played in more than 200 countries.

More than 4,000 years ago, ancient Greeks played the football-like game episkyros. Teams kicked the ball and used their hands to score goals.

In ancient China, soldiers played a game like football called Ts'u-chü or Cuju. They kicked a leather ball into a net.

Early footballs were made from inflated pig's bladders and strips of leather.

In 1863, the Football Association (FA) created football's first official rules.

The first women's football teams formed in the late 1880s in the UK.

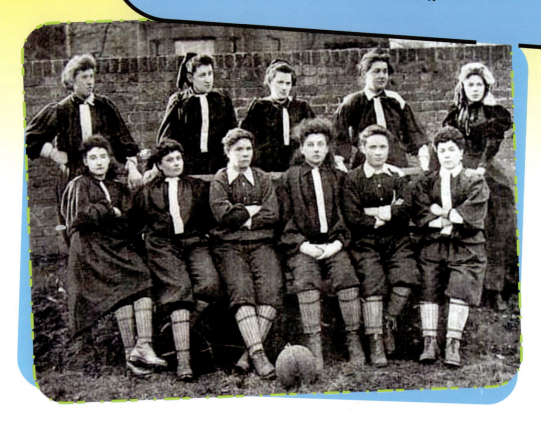

In 1904, FA members formed the Federation Internationale de Football Association (FIFA). FIFA organizes the World Cup and other major international **tournaments**.

England played Scotland in the first international football match in 1872.

More people watch football in person and on TV than any other sport.

In Canada, the United States and Australia, football is called soccer.

Chapter 2

Playing on a pitch

A football match is played on a **pitch**. Players try to put the ball into the other team's net to score. The team with the highest number of goals at the end of the game wins.

The pitch is usually grass. Artificial grass is rarely used in professional games.

A goal is scored when the ball crosses the other team's goal line between the goal posts and under the **crossbar**.

Each football team has 11 players on the pitch at a time.

A **header** is using the head to pass the ball or aim it into the goal.

Cristiano Ronaldo once jumped 2.9 metres to head the ball into the goal!

Players can touch the ball with their feet, legs, body and head. Only the goalkeepers can use their hands.

The bicycle kick is an amazing move in which a player moves their upper body backwards and pedals the legs to strike the ball in mid-air.

Referees make sure players are following the rules. They watch for **fouls**.

A yellow card from the referee is a warning for a player's misconduct.

A red card means a player must leave the pitch immediately and is not replaced.

Chapter 3

Players and positions

Each player has an important job to do. The four main positions are goalkeeper, defender, midfielder and forward.

Forwards score the most goals. The centre forward is called the striker.

Midfielders play between the forwards and defenders.

Midfielders run up and down the pitch. Sometimes they run more than 11 km in a match!

Defenders block attacking forwards.

The goalkeeper keeps balls out of the goal.

Goalkeeper Briana Scurry played for the US women's national team. In 2017, she was inducted into the National Soccer Hall of Fame.

13

When the goalkeeper keeps the other team from scoring any goals in a match, it's called a clean sheet. Goalkeeper Petr Čech holds the record for the most clean sheets in Premier League history.

A player's kit is a shirt, shorts, shin guards, knee-high socks and football boots.

Goalkeepers wear gloves to protect their hands and grip the ball.

Goalkeepers wear a different colour kit from the rest of their team and the opposing team.

Star forward Marta Vieira da Silva became the first footballer to score in five straight Olympic Games.

15

Chapter 4

Teams

Most communities have youth clubs and teams. Many people play at school, college or university. A few play professionally and earn money.

There are about 3,900 professional clubs. Mexico has the most with more than 260.

Real Madrid was named the best football club of the 20th century by FIFA.

Some teams have famous **rivalries** such as the one between Real Madrid and FC Barcelona.

Most professional clubs run youth academies to identify and train players starting from the age of 6. At 13, the best players can stay.

Argentinian superstar Lionel Messi was **scouted** for FC Barcelona's famous La Masia youth academy at 13 years old.

In 2022, midfielder Maximo Carrizo became the youngest player to sign a contract with MLS in the United States at the age of 14.

Countries select their best players for their national team.

Brazil has the most successful men's national team.

18

The United States has the most successful women's national team.

The club that has won the most trophies is Egypt's Al Ahly with 188.

Chapter 5

Fans and stadiums

Football fans shout and sing to cheer on their favourite teams. They're proud of their team and show support in many ways.

In the 1930s, football fans in the UK started wearing knitted scarves in team colours. Today, football scarves are still popular.

The vuvuzela is a popular cheering horn at South African matches. But it was so loud at the 2010 World Cup that it was **banned** from future World Cups.

The Maracanã Stadium in Brazil set a record for the most people ever at a football match during the 1950 World Cup. It held 173,850 people!

Nef Stadium in Turkey holds the record for the loudest crowd roar. The crowd of 52,044 fans was as loud as a jet taking off.

Before a match, professional teams enter a stadium with youth players who are specially chosen.

One of the largest stadiums is Nou Camp in Barcelona, Spain. It holds 99,354 people.

The shape of the First National Bank (FNB) Stadium in Johannesburg, South Africa, was inspired by traditional African pots called calabashes.

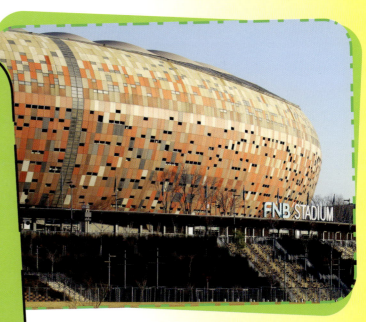

You can only get to Ottmar Hitzfeld Gspon Arena, Switzerland, by cable car because it is 2,000 metres above sea level.

The outside of the Allianz Arena in Munich, Germany, has 3,000 panels that change colour.

23

Chapter 6

Mascots and nicknames

Mascots add to the fun of a game.
Many teams have fun nicknames too.

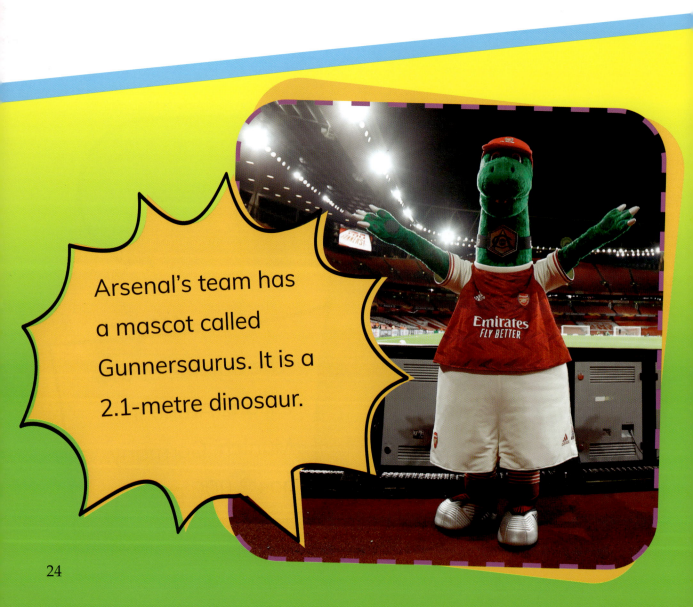

Arsenal's team has a mascot called Gunnersaurus. It is a 2.1-metre dinosaur.

Germany's FC Cologne mascot is a live billy goat.

Spain's Villarreal CF nickname is "Yellow Submarine" from the Beatles song and their team colour.

On 4 July 2016, the LA Galaxy's mascot Cozmo jumped out of a plane and parachuted into the StubHub Center in California.

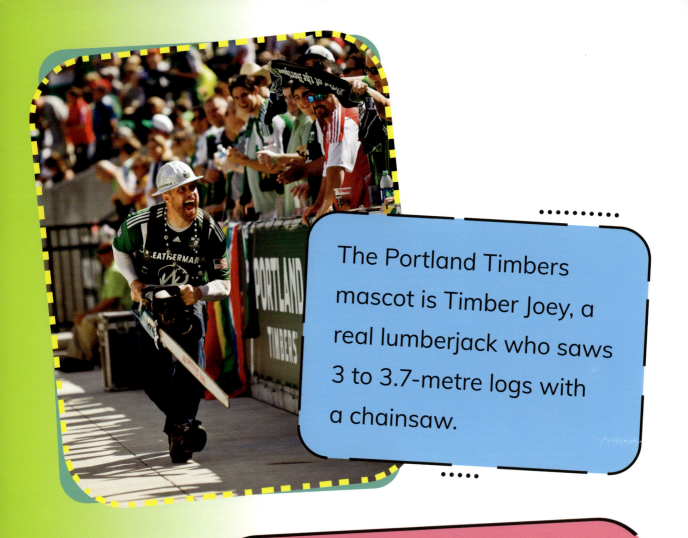

The Portland Timbers mascot is Timber Joey, a real lumberjack who saws 3 to 3.7-metre logs with a chainsaw.

Japan's national team nickname is the Samurai Blue after the players' deep blue uniforms.

Australia's national team nickname, Socceroos, is a combination of the words "soccer" and "kangaroos".

The Netherlands national team is known as Clockwork Orange. Fans wear orange and their mascot is an orange lion.

Brazil's national team has a yellow canary mascot with an angry face. Its face shows the frustration of fans after losing the World Cup in 2014.

Chapter 7

The World Cup

The FIFA World Cup is one of the largest competitions in world sport. Held every four years, countries participate with their national team.

The first World Cup was held in 1930 in Uruguay.

The Women's World Cup is held the year after the Men's World Cup.

The first Women's World Cup was held in 1991 in China.

Nearly half the world, 3.57 billion people, watched the 2018 World Cup on TV.

The highest-scoring game in World Cup history took place in 1954. Austria beat Switzerland 7–5.

The 2002 World Cup was the first to be hosted by two countries. Both South Korea and Japan hosted it.

The winners of the World Cup receive a large gold trophy.

Banned items at World Cups have included selfie sticks, tablets, cameras, inflatable balls, umbrellas and chewing gum.

The FIFAe World Cup is a large online e-sports tournament. Gamers compete to win prize money.

Glossary

ban not allow

crossbar bar that connects to both posts of the goal

foul action that is against the rules

header shot or pass in football using the head

pitch grass area that a football match is played on

rivalry fierce feeling of competition between two teams

scout look for players who might be able to join a team

tournament series of matches between several players or teams, ending with one winner

Index

Carrizo, Maximo 18
Cech, Petr 14

defenders 12

Federation Internationale de Football Association (FIFA) 6, 16, 28
FIFAe World Cup 30
forwards 12, 13, 15
fouls 11

goalkeepers 10, 12, 13, 14, 15
goals 4, 8, 12, 14

headers 9

mascots 24, 25, 26, 27
Messi, Lionel 17
midfielders 12, 13, 18

referees 11
Ronaldo, Cristiano 9

Scurry, Briana 13
Silva, Marta Vieira da 15

World Cup 6, 21, 27, 28, 30

photo credit: Di Starr Studios

About the author

Colette Weil Parrinello is a writer, runner and avid reader. She loves sport and the outdoors. She lives under the majestic redwoods in Northern California, USA, and can be seen running the paths along the marsh and bay.